Now You're COOKING

HEALTHY RECIPES FROM
LATIN AMERICA

PUERTO RICO

Amie Jane Leavitt

PURPLE TOAD
PUBLISHING

P.O. Box 631
Kennett Square, Pennsylvania 19348
www.purpletoadpublishing.com

Now You're COOKING
HEALTHY RECIPES FROM
LATIN AMERICA

Brazil

Cuba

Guatemala

Mexico

Puerto Rico

PUBLISHER'S NOTE: The data in this book has been researched in depth, and to the best of our knowledge is factual. Although every measure is taken to give an accurate account, Purple Toad Publishing makes no warranty of the accuracy of the information and is not liable for damages caused by inaccuracies.

Printing   1   2   3   4   5   6   7   8   9

Publisher's Cataloging-in-Publication Data
Leavitt, Amie Jane
  Puerto Rico / Amie Jane Leavitt
    p. cm. – (Now you're cooking. Healthy recipes from Latin America)
Includes bibliographic references and index.
ISBN: 978-1-62469-004-4 (library bound)
1..Cooking, Puerto Rican. 2. Cooking – Juvenile literature. 3. Recipes for health.   I. Title.
 TX716.P8L43 2013
  641.5972'95—dc23
                                          2013930993

eBook ISBN: 978-1-62469-015-0

Printed by Lake Book Manufacturing, Chicago, IL

CONTENTS

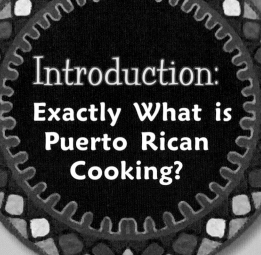

Introduction:
Exactly What is Puerto Rican Cooking?

¡Hola! Welcome to Puerto Rico! This beautiful tropical island is located between the North Atlantic Ocean and the aqua blue waters of the Caribbean Sea. It is just east of the Dominican Republic and west of the Virgin Islands. Puerto Rico is part of the Greater Antilles (Cuba, Jamaica, Dominican Republic, and Haiti). Since 1898, it has been a territory of the United States.

Christopher Columbus was the first European to land on the island of Puerto Rico. He did so during his second voyage to the New World in November 1493. The island wasn't named Puerto Rico by Columbus. It actually received this name later on when gold was found in one of the rivers. In Spanish, *Puerto Rico* means "rich port." To locals the island is also known as "Isla del Encanto" which in Spanish means "island of enchantment."

The Taíno were the native peoples who were living here when Columbus arrived. They were an agricultural society, which meant they grew crops, raised animals for food, and occasionally fished and hunted, too. They grew corn, yams, peanuts, taro, and cassava in their fields. They gathered food from plants that grew wild on the island, such as lima beans, black-eyed peas, guava, pineapple, soursop, and seagrapes. For meat, the Taíno ate reptiles, including iguanas and turtles. They also ate birds and seafood.

Puerto Rico is a lush, green tropical island teeming with colorful flowers, fruits, and rain forest plants.

Puerto Rico

Atlantic Ocean

Parque Indígena de Caguana

Rincón

Arecibo

San Juan

El Yunque

Mayagüez

Utuado

Bayamón

Carolina

Isla de Culebra

Cerro La Punta

San Germán

Cordillera Central

Caguas

Cabo Rojo

Ponce

Fajardo

Bosque Estatal de Guánica

Guayama

Isla de Vieques

Esperanza

Caribbean Sea

30 mi

Since Columbus's arrival more than 500 years ago, many people from throughout the world have come to live in Puerto Rico. With them, they have brought their own traditional recipes and ingredients from other areas.

The Spanish came first. They brought with them a variety of foods from Europe and from the other places where they had traveled. They brought papaya from Central America, mangoes and tamarind from India, citrus fruits, eggplant, onion, cilantro, garlic, olives, chickpeas, and pomegranates from Spain. They brought potatoes from the Andes, cocoa and avocados from Mexico, and breadfruit from Tahiti.

The African slaves brought plantains, bananas, coconuts, pigeon peas, and yucca. They also brought with them the technique of frying food. The Dutch brought cheese. The Italians brought pasta and chicken. The Chinese brought dumplings.

As you will see from the recipes in this book, all of these ingredients and ways of cooking have blended together to create the unique cuisine that is found in Puerto Rico. This type of cuisine is called *Cocina Criolla*.

Cocina Criolla is similar to the cuisines of Puerto Rico's closest island neighbors, Cuba, the Dominican Republic, Haiti, Jamaica, and the Virgin Islands. Yet even though there are similarities, each island has its own unique style. Overall, the flavors of food that are found in this Caribbean region really are found nowhere else on earth.

So, let's get started. Turn on some Puerto Rican tunes and let's get cooking. When you're all done and you sit down to dive into your feast, it'll feel like you've just taken a trip to this beautiful island. *¡Delicioso!*

Breakfast
Puerto Rican Style

In many places, breakfast is considered the most important meal of the day. Puerto Rico is no different. Puerto Ricans call breakfast *desayuno.* It ranges from hot or cold cereal to heartier dishes like a potato and egg omelet. Recipes for these breakfast specialties are found on pages 10–13.

In addition to these dishes, Puerto Ricans enjoy eating sandwiches for breakfast. Generally, the sandwiches are served hot and are similar to a loaded grilled cheese or panini. To make them, you first take two slices of French bread and spread on either mayonnaise or butter. Then, you layer on your choice of meats, cheese, lettuce, and tomato. The sandwich is either grilled in a pan and pressed down with a spatula after flipping or it's made in a special sandwich press. Either way, the result is a crispy, hot, pressed sandwich that adds a jumpstart to your day.

Many Puerto Rican breakfasts also include a cup of *chocolate caliente,* or hot chocolate. Puerto Ricans make their hot chocolate a little differently than in other places. Believe it or not, they actually add several small cubes of cheddar cheese to the drink. Not sure if you'll like it this way? The only way to find out is to give it a try. Drink up!

Funche

Breakfast Cornmeal Hot Cereal

Funche is a traditional Puerto Rican dish. When the Europeans settled in Puerto Rico, they brought some of their traditional hot cereal recipes. In their own countries, they would have used types of grain like wheat or oats that were available to them to make their hot cereal. Since corn was available in the New World, they started using cornmeal in their cereal. Thus, the creamy cereal called *funche* was born.

Ingredients

1½	cups fine-grained cornmeal
1½	cups water
1½	cups milk
1–2	tablespoons butter
	honey, to taste
	cubed pineapple, mango, or banana

Directions

1. With the help of an **adult,** bring the water, milk, butter, and a pinch of salt to a boil.
2. Remove from heat.
3. Slowly add the cornmeal, stirring constantly until well mixed.
4. Drizzle on honey until it is as sweet as you would like it.
5. Return to heat and keep stirring constantly until the cereal has thickened.

Scoop into bowls and top with more milk, honey, and cubed fruit. Makes 4 servings.

> Corn is also called maize. This is considered America's first crop. Ancient peoples in South America, Central America, and North America ate this grain as their main food source. Many of the people who live in this area today still do.

Tortilla Española
Potato and Egg Omelet

In Mexican cooking, a tortilla is a flat bread made out of flour or cornmeal. In Puerto Rican cooking, a tortilla is a puffed dish similar to an omelet. Whereas Mexican tortillas are served rolled up, folded over, or fried with ingredients inside (as in burritos, tacos, or chimichangas), a Puerto Rican tortilla is served in a wedge or triangle like a slice of pie or cake. Most Puerto Rican tortillas are made to be savory and not sweet.

This Puerto Rican tortilla is actually a traditional tortilla from Spain. The dish was most likely introduced to the island when Spanish colonists settled there hundreds of years ago.

Ingredients

1 12-ounce bag frozen cubed potatoes, thawed
2 tablespoons olive oil
1 medium onion (white or yellow), sliced thin
1 teaspoon salt
½ teaspoon pepper (optional)
6 eggs, well beaten

Directions

1. With the help of an **adult,** preheat oven to 375°F.
2. Then, in a large non-stick skillet (at least 12 inches in diameter), heat the olive oil on the stovetop on medium heat.
3. Add onions and cook until they begin to turn golden brown.
4. Spray a 2-quart casserole dish with cooking spray.
5. Arrange the potatoes and onions in the bottom of the dish.
6. Slowly pour the beaten eggs on top of the potatoes and onions.
7. Bake for 30 to 35 minutes.

Serve warm with a side of fresh fruit, if desired.
Makes 8 servings.

Baked Tostones

If you were to ask a Puerto Rican what the most typical part of a traditional meal is, he or she would most likely answer "tostones." Tostones are fried plantain chips or fritters that are served with just about every meal. For this dish, the tostones will be made in a healthy way. They will be baked, not fried.

A plantain is a fruit that looks very similar to a banana. If fruits had family members, the plantain would be the banana's cousin. Plantains range from green (unripe) to black (very ripe), just like a banana. Yet, they are larger and firmer than bananas. For this recipe, you will use green unripe plantains.

Ingredients

3   medium green plantains
2   teaspoons olive oil
    salt
    cooking spray
    waxed paper
    a drinking glass

Directions

1. With the help of an **adult,** preheat the oven to 400°F.
2. Remove the peels from the plantains and discard.
3. Cut plantains into ¼-inch slices.
4. Place in a bowl.
5. Pour olive oil and salt on top of the slices. Stir until all of the plantains are coated.
6. Spray a baking sheet with cooking spray.
7. Arrange the slices on the baking sheet.
8. Lightly spray the plantains with the cooking spray.
9. Bake for 10 minutes or until the bottoms are slightly brown.
10. Remove from the oven. Let cool slightly.
11. Lay the plantains out on a piece of waxed paper. Place another piece of waxed paper on top.
12. Use a drinking glass to press down on each plantain to flatten.

Tostones are also called "plantain fritters."

13. Remove them from the waxed paper. Place the plantains brown-side up onto the baking sheets.
14. Bake for another 15 minutes or until golden brown and crispy.

Serve as an appetizer with any of the meals in this book! Or just eat them plain. They're yummy no matter how you serve them. You can also use these to make the plantain sandwich on page 22. You'll just need to slice them lengthwise instead of into rounds.

Makes 4 servings.

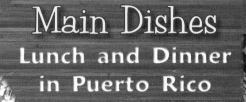

Main Dishes
Lunch and Dinner in Puerto Rico

In Puerto Rico, lunch generally starts around 11 a.m. and lasts until 2 p.m. These hours are similar to those in the United States. After lunch, between 2 p.m. and 4 p.m., many adults will have their second cup of coffee for the day (the first was with breakfast). In the United States, oftentimes coffee drinkers will drink several cups throughout the day.

Dinner can start as early as 5:30 p.m.; however, most people don't start their evening meal until much later, around 7 p.m. This is just like it is in Spain and other European countries. In fact, South American countries such as Argentina, Brazil, and Uruguay follow this tradition, too.

People usually dress up for dinner. They never wear beach clothes to restaurants—that kind of attire is only for the beach. Oftentimes men wear jackets and ties and women wear dresses.

When people go to restaurants, they don't just eat and run as many people do in the United States. Instead, they eat and talk and eat and talk. Most of the time, the talking and eating go on for hours, making dinners last until around 11 p.m. If you were to reserve a table at a restaurant, you would be expected to stay at that table for the majority of the night. In the United States, servers often expect customers to leave the table shortly after they have finished their meals.

It is easy to see why outdoor dining is popular in Puerto Rico.

Asopao de Pollo:
Chicken and Rice Stew

Asopao is a Spanish word for a stew that is thickened with rice. This particular dish has pimiento-stuffed green olives and capers, which are popular in Spanish cooking. Brown rice is used here instead of white rice to make the dish healthier.

Ingredients

1	tablespoon olive oil
1	4-ounce can chopped green chilies, drained
1	small onion, chopped
1	tablespoon dried oregano
1	teaspoon sweet paprika
1	teaspoon sea salt
2	cups raw chicken, cut into cubes
1	8-ounce can tomato sauce
1	tomato, chopped
1	4-ounce jar pimientos
8	pimiento-stuffed green olives, sliced
2	tablespoons capers
8	cups water
2½	cups brown rice
⅔	cup fresh cilantro, chopped

Directions

1. Place oil, green chilies, onion, oregano, paprika, salt, and chicken in a deep sauce pan.
2. With the help of an **adult,** cook on medium-high on the stovetop until onion is clear and soft. This will take about 3 to 5 minutes.
3. Add the tomato sauce, tomato, pimientos, olives, capers, and water. Heat until it boils, stirring constantly.
4. Stir in the rice. Return mixture to a boil. Then reduce heat.

Asopao de Pollo

5. Continue cooking, uncovered, until the rice is tender and the chicken is cooked all the way through. Stir as needed so it doesn't burn. It will take about 35 to 45 minutes for the chicken and rice to finish cooking.
6. To serve, scoop into individual bowls and sprinkle with cilantro.

Serve warm on a plate with a side of fresh fruit, if desired.
Makes 8 servings.

Mojo Isleño

The name of this dish means "islander sauce." It is very popular on the Caribbean side of Puerto Rico in a little town called Salinas. The people make this dish throughout the year here, but especially in July during their Festival del Mojo Isleño. Traditionally, the people use Red Snapper in the dish, but any fish with white meat can be used, such as tilapia, cod, or grouper.

Ingredients

¼ cup olive oil
1 onion, chopped
1 Anaheim chili pepper, chopped (or a green bell pepper if you'd like it less spicy)
4–6 cloves of garlic, minced
2 cups tomatoes, diced (or a 15-ounce can diced tomatoes, drained)
2 tablespoons lime juice
¼ cup pimento-stuffed green olives, chopped
1 tablespoon capers, rinsed
1–2 bay leaves
2 pounds fish fillets, cut into serving portions
sea salt and fresh ground black pepper to taste

Directions

1. With the help of an **adult,** heat olive oil in a sauce pan over medium heat. Sauté onions and peppers until they look transparent or clear.
2. Add garlic and sauté for 1 to 2 minutes more.
3. Add tomatoes, lime juice, olives, capers, and bay leaves.
4. Simmer 10 to 12 minutes.
5. Heat a non-stick skillet to medium-high heat. Coat the bottom of the skillet with olive oil.
6. Salt and pepper the fish fillets.
7. Then, place them in the skillet and cook until lightly browned on both sides.
8. Cook until they are 145° F, when tested in the center with a meat thermometer.

The Festival del Mojo Isleño features hometown music and Mojo Isleño.

9. Use a spatula to place the fish fillets onto plates and then top them with the sauce.

Serve warm on a plate with a side of fresh fruit, if desired.
Makes 8 servings.

Sandwich de Plátano:
Plantain Sandwich

In old town San Juan, little roadside shacks called *kioskos* are set up along the city streets. These stands sell all sorts of lunch fare, including sandwiches that use tostones in place of bread. They're a quick meal that can be made at home just as easily as at a kiosoko. In fact, these sandwiches are popular in Chicago, thanks to a restaurant owner named Juan C. Figueroa. He started serving what he calls the jibarito, in 1996. His customers love them. Juan sells hundreds of plantain sandwiches every day.

Ingredients

2   tostones (this will be the "bread" for the sandwich; see page 14 for the recipe)
1   thin slice of your favorite cheese (American, cheddar, provolone, mozzarella)
2   slices of turkey breast or grilled chicken
1   slice tomato
    lettuce
    garlic mayo (recipe below)

Directions

1. Make the garlic mayo by mixing 1 cup mayonnaise, ½ teaspoon chili powder, ½ teaspoon ground cumin, 1 clove of garlic (minced with a garlic press), dash of sea salt and freshly ground black pepper.
2. Lightly spread the garlic mayo on one side of each of the tostones.
3. Now, build the sandwich by adding the cheese, ham, tomatoes, and lettuce on one of the tostones. Then, top with the other tostone.

Makes 1 small sandwich. You can even use peanut butter instead of the poultry, cheese and vegetables.

Plantain sandwich with grilled chicken

Habichuelas Coloradas Grandes:
Island Red Beans

Beans are a staple in traditional island cuisine because of the protein and fiber they provide. Meat wasn't always available. When it was available, sometimes it was too expensive to buy. Yet beans were always plentiful.

Many different types of beans are eaten on the island. There are pink beans, red beans, black beans, pigeon peas, chickpeas, and kidney beans. All are equally delicious and beloved in traditional island cuisine.

Ingredients

½   tablespoon olive oil
2   cloves garlic, minced with garlic press
1   4-ounce can chopped green chilies, drained
1   small onion, chopped
¼   cup cilantro, chopped
2   15-ounce cans red kidney beans, drained and rinsed
¼   cup tomato sauce
¼   teaspoon dried oregano
⅛   teaspoon freshly ground black pepper
⅛   teaspoon sea salt
1–3 cups water

Directions

1. Heat oil in a deep saucepan over medium-high heat.
2. Add garlic, chilies, onion, and cilantro.
3. Cook until the onion is clear and soft. Stir constantly so it doesn't burn.
4. Add beans, tomato sauce, oregano, salt, and pepper.
5. Add water. The water should cover the ingredients by at least 1 inch.

Bean fields (background) contribute to a favorite dish in Puerto Rico, beans and rice.

6. Bring the mixture to a boil. Then, reduce heat and simmer for 30 minutes. Stir occasionally.

Serve plain or mixed with hot rice. Garnish with chopped cilantro if desired.

Makes 4 servings.

Arroz con Gandules:
Yellow Rice with Pigeon Peas

Yellow rice with pigeon peas, or *arroz con gandules,* is considered by many to be Puerto Rico's national dish. In fact, yellow rice is still popular in Spain. Yellow tumeric, a spice, was brought to Puerto Rico by Spanish colonists, whereas the pigeon pea is native to Africa. It was, and still is, an important food source for people who live in that area of the world.

In Puerto Rico, *arroz con gandules* is served for Christmas and other special occasions throughout the year. At Christmastime, it is served with roasted turkey.

Ingredients

1   tablespoon olive oil
1   small onion, chopped
2   cloves garlic, minced with garlic press
3   cups brown rice
1   teaspoon sea salt
1   teaspoon freshly ground black pepper
1   tablespoon turmeric
1   15-ounce can pigeon peas
1   can of coconut milk
3   cups chicken broth

Directions

1. Place oil, onion, and garlic in a deep saucepan. With the help of an **adult,** cook on medium-high heat until onion is clear and soft.
2. Add the rice, salt, pepper, and turmeric. Cook until everything is coated with the yellow turmeric.
3. Add coconut milk, chicken broth, and peas.
4. Turn the temperature down to low. Cover the pot with a lid. Let the mixture simmer until the water is absorbed. This should take about 40 to 45 minutes. If any water is left, keep the pot covered and the rice cooking until the water has been completely absorbed.

The pigeon pea plant has red and yellow flowers. The legumes it produces are used to make *Arroz con Gandules.*

Fluff with a fork and serve. Eat plain or along with the meat, soup, sandwich, or salad recipes in this book.
Makes 6 to 8 servings.

Sopa de Plátanos:
Plantain Soup

In traditional Puerto Rican cuisine, formal lunch and dinner meals always begin with soup. Serving formal meals isn't common anymore. Yet, even so, soups are still an important part of Puerto Rican cuisine. Soups are usually served as a meal all by themselves.

Sopa de plátanos combines the tasty plantain with chicken stock, cilantro, garlic, and Parmesan cheese. To top it off, add a lime and avocado to each bowl. These last two ingredients give the soup a particular island flavor.

Ingredients

3   green plantains, peeled
1   teaspoon olive oil
2   cloves garlic, minced with garlic press
½   cup fresh cilantro, chopped
8   cups chicken broth
1½ cups water
½   teaspoon sea salt
     freshly ground black pepper, to taste
8   teaspoons finely shredded Parmesan cheese
8   lime wedges
8   avocado wedges

Directions

1. Use a box grater and shred the plantains.
2. With the help of an **adult,** place oil, garlic, and half of the cilantro in a deep sauce pan. On medium-high heat, cook until the garlic is softened. This should take about 1 to 2 minutes.
3. Add chicken broth and water.
4. Bring the mixture to a boil.
5. Stir in the plantains.

Plantain soup

6. Reduce heat. Simmer until the plantains are tender and the soup is thickened. This should take about 30 minutes.
7. Stir in the other half of the cilantro and the salt and pepper. Scoop the soup into individual bowls. Sprinkle each bowl with 1 tablespoon Parmesan cheese. Then, add a lime wedge and an avocado wedge to each.

Makes 8 servings.

Bacalao:
Puerto Rican
Fish Stew

Puerto Rico is an island in the Caribbean Sea, so seafood is naturally an important part of the local cuisine. Some of the most popular seafood in Puerto Rico is caught locally and includes Puerto Rican Red Snapper, clams, cod, conch, marlin, salmon, spiny lobster, tuna, West Indian Great Land Crab, oysters, mussels, and shrimp.

For this recipe, any white fish fillets will do, such as haddock, tilapia, or cod. Use whatever is available in your area.

Ingredients

2   tablespoons olive oil
1   medium onion, chopped
4   cloves garlic, minced with garlic press
1   pound white fish fillets (haddock, tilapia, cod), cut into 1½-inch
     pieces
1   14-ounce can diced tomatoes
1   can chopped green chilies, drained
¼   cup fresh cilantro, chopped
2   tablespoons sliced pimiento-stuffed green olives
1   tablespoon capers
1   teaspoon oregano
½   teaspoon salt
½   cup water

Serve warm on a plate with a side of fresh fruit, if desired. Makes 4 servings.

Directions

1. Place the oil, onion, and garlic in a deep sauce pan. With the help of an **adult,** cook on medium high heat until the onion is clear and soft.
2. Add fish, tomatoes, chilies, cilantro, olives, capers, oregano, salt, and water. Stir to combine.
3. Turn down heat to low. Cover and simmer for 20 minutes.

Bacalao

Sopa de Frijoles Negros:
Black Bean Soup

Black beans are popular in Latin American and Caribbean cuisine. They are also known as turtle beans, Spanish beans, and Tampico beans. It is believed that this bean originated in Mexico more than 7,000 years ago. How do we know this? Well, these types of beans have been found preserved inside prehistoric dwellings.

Like all other beans, black beans are high in protein. They are also a good source of fiber and are loaded with vitamins.

This soup can be served by itself or on top of rice. Either way, it makes for a hearty side dish, starter, or meal.

Ingredients
1 tablespoon olive oil
1 cup onion, chopped (about 1 small onion)
4 cloves garlic, minced with garlic press
¾ cup diced carrots (about 2 medium carrots)
¾ cup diced celery (about 2 stalks of celery)
2 15-ounce cans black beans, drained and rinsed
1 14-ounce can chopped green chilies
1 28-ounce can chicken broth
1 tablespoon sea salt
⅛ teaspoon freshly ground black pepper
½ teaspoon chili powder
¼ teaspoon cumin
½ teaspoon dry oregano
1 bay leaf

Directions
1. In a deep saucepan, place the oil, onion, and garlic. With the help of an **adult,** cook on medium-high heat until the onion is clear and soft.
2. Add carrots and celery. Cook for 4 to 5 minutes.
3. Add black beans, chilies, and chicken broth. Stir to combine.
4. Add salt and pepper, chili powder, cumin, oregano, and the bay leaf.

Black bean soup

5. Turn heat to low. Simmer uncovered for 20 to 25 minutes or until the carrots are tender.
6. Remove from heat.
7. Use a spoon to remove the bay leaf.

Serve warm.
Makes 6 servings.

Green Banana Salad

At picnics in the United States, you might find a traditional potato salad. In Puerto Rico, you will likely find a similar salad that is made with green bananas instead of spuds. This salad combines fruit (bananas), vegetables (peppers), and seafood (crab and shrimp) to make it true island picnic fare. This salad can be served as a side for lunch or dinner with rice, beans, and a meat dish. Or it can be served on its own with a side of tostones.

Ingredients

6   small green bananas
2   tablespoons olive oil
1   cup small shrimp, ready to eat
1   cup crabmeat
1   green bell pepper, sliced into thin rings
1   small onion, chopped
¼   teaspoon sea salt
¼   teaspoon freshly ground black pepper
1   teaspoon honey
¾   cup apple cider vinegar

Directions

1. With the help of an **adult,** fill a medium pot with water. Bring to a boil on high heat.
2. Cut the ends off the bananas. Then, cut a slit lengthwise in each peel. Place the bananas (with the peels still on) in the boiling water. Cook until tender.
3. Drain the bananas in a colander. Let cool. Then, remove the peels.
4. Cut the bananas into small chunks. Place in a serving bowl.
5. Drizzle the bananas with 1 tablespoon of olive oil. Stir so that they are all lightly coated with the oil. Set aside.
6. In a medium skillet, heat the remaining oil on medium-high heat. Add the shrimp and crab meat. Fry until cooked thoroughly. This should take about 5 minutes. Set aside and let cool.

7. Add the onions, green peppers, and seafood to the bananas in the bowl.
8. To make the dressing, mix the apple cider vinegar and honey in a small bowl. Pour this mixture over the banana mixture. Toss gently so everything is coated with it. Season with salt and pepper.

Serve on a bed of mixed salad greens. Even capers and peppers can be added. Add slices of hard-boiled egg if you'd like.
Makes 6 servings.

Banana Coconut Treat

Bananas and coconuts were brought to Puerto Rico from Africa. Ever since, these two fruits have been important to Puerto Rican cuisine. Bananas and their cousins (the plantains) are used just about daily in a variety of ways. Coconuts are used either for their flaked meat or milk.

Ingredients
2   yellow bananas (Ripe, but not too ripe. The bananas should be yellow, not green, and have no black marks.)
1   orange
2   cups coconut shavings

Directions
1. Peel the bananas.
2. Cut tiny slices off the ends.
3. Cut the orange in half. Squeeze the juice onto the bananas. This will help the coconut stick to them.
4. Roll the bananas in the coconut shavings.

Serve.
Makes 2 servings.

Freeze them for extra fun!

Sticks in the
bananas are
optional!

Banana
Ice Cream

Ingredients

3 to 4 very ripe bananas
4   cups milk
4   tablespoons honey
½   teaspoon vanilla extract

Directions

1. Mix the bananas, milk, honey, and vanilla extract in a blender.
2. Pour into plastic disposable cups and freeze.

Serve.
Makes 4 servings.
(Variation: To make coconut ice cream, replace the ripe bananas with a 15-ounce can of coconut milk.)

Banana ice cream

Traditional Puerto Rican Flan

Flan is a traditional Spanish dessert. This custard dish is found in former Spanish colonies, such as the Philippines and in Latin America. It has a similar texture to pumpkin pie.

Flan can be made in many flavors: caramel (like this recipe), mango, pineapple, coconut, chocolate, pumpkin, and strawberry. Some people are known to hold on with a firm grip to their grandmother's recipe for flan and only pass it on to the luckiest of their immediate family members.

This caramel custard dish is made with sugar, eggs, and milk. To make it healthier, this recipe calls for Sucanat whole cane sugar. The taste will be the same.

Ingredients

½ cup plus ⅔ cup Sucanat whole cane sugar
3 whole eggs
3 egg yolks
3 cups milk
2 teaspoons vanilla extract

Directions

1. Preheat the oven to 350°F.
2. Cook ½ cup Sucanat whole cane sugar over medium heat in a medium-sized sauce pan. Stir constantly. Cook until the sucanat is melted and turns a dark brown color. This should take 5 minutes. Be careful with this step since cooked sugar is very hot. Have an **adult** help you. Pour this sugar into a 2-quart baking dish.
3. In a mixing bowl, whisk the eggs, egg yolks, and the remaining ⅔ cup of Sucanat whole cane sugar. Whisk until the mixture is smooth.
4. Add the milk and vanilla.
5. Pour this milk mixture over the sugar in the dish.
6. Find a larger baking dish. Place this smaller milk-filled dish inside the larger dish. Then, carefully add water to the larger dish.

Puerto Rican flan

7. Have an adult help you place these two dishes in the oven.
8. Bake for 35 to 45 minutes or until a butter knife inserted into the center comes out clean.
9. When you remove it from the oven, with the help of an adult, you will need to place the smaller dish in another dish that is filled with ice cold water. This will help the flan stop cooking! Once the flan is cooled, refrigerate it for at least 1 hour before you serve it.

Serve with a side of fresh fruit, if desired.
Makes 8 servings.

Arroz con Dulce:
Coconut Rice Pudding

Many Puerto Ricans make coconut rice for the perfect ending to their annual Christmas Eve dinner. But don't let that stop you from making it at other times of the year. It is a delicious treat any time.

Ingredients

6   cups coconut milk, divided
1   cup uncooked brown rice
6   cinnamon sticks
¼   teaspoon ground ginger
1¼ teaspoons sea salt
1   cup Sucanat whole cane sugar or honey
1   cup seedless raisins

Directions

1. In a deep saucepan, place 5 cups of the coconut milk and the rice. Let it soak for 2½ hours.
2. After it soaks, add cinnamon sticks, ginger, and salt to the pan.
3. With the help of an **adult,** cook covered on low heat for about 30 to 35 minutes. Do not stir.
4. Add Sucanat or honey, the rest of the coconut milk, and raisins.
5. Continue cooking for another 40 to 45 minutes until the rice is soft.
6. This time, stir every 10 minutes or so to prevent the mixture from sticking to the pan.

Serve in individual bowls with cinnamon and honey sprinkled on top. Milk or coconut milk can also be added.

Makes 6 servings.

Arroz con dulce

Books

Baker, Christopher. *Top 10 Puerto Rico* (Eyewitness Top Ten Travel Guide). New York: DK Publishing, 2011.

Lindroth, David. *Let's Go: Puerto Rico.* Cambridge, MA: Let's Go, Inc., 2006.

Works Consulted:

Gutner, Howard. *Puerto Rico: A True Book.* New York: Scholastic Library Publishing, 2009.

Marcus, Amy. *Exploring Puerto Rico with the Five Themes of Geography.* New York: Rosen Publishing Group, 2005.

Reynolds, Jeff E. *A to Z: Puerto Rico.* New York: Children's Press, 2004.

Taqliaferro, Linda. *Puerto Rico in Pictures.* Minneapolis: Lerner Publishing Group, 2003.

Zapata, Elizabeth. *Read About Geography: Puerto Rico.* New York: Scholastic, 2007.

On the Internet

Black Beans: The American Treasure
> http://www.beanbible.com/modules.php?op=modload&name=Ne
> ws&file=article&sid=23&mode=thread&order=0&thold=0

El Boricua
> http://www.elboricua.com/PuertoRican101.html

Borinquen: Chicago Puerto Rican Restaurant
> http://www.borinquenoncalifornia.net/

Chicken and Rice Recipe – Arroz con Pollo
> http://spanishfood.about.com/od/maincourses/r/arrozconpollo.htm

El Jibarito (Plantain and Steak Sandwich)
> http://thenoshery.com/2009/06/08/
> el-jibarito-plantain-and-steak-sandwich/

Growing Pigeon Peas
> http://www.tropicalpermaculture.com/pigeon-pea.html

Party With Pig: In Puerto Rico, a Glorious Feast
> http://www.nytimes.com/2007/07/04/dining/04lech.
> html?pagewanted=all&_moc.semityn.www

Plantain Sandwich
> http://www.thehealthyhousewife.com/2011/09/plantain-sandwich/

Puerto Rican Hot Chocolate
> http://www.youtube.com/watch?v=uZgaxn-D4Co

Puerto Rico – History and Heritage
> http://www.smithsonianmag.com/travel/destination-hunter/north-
> america/caribbean-atlantic/puerto-rico/puerto-rico-history-heritage.
> html

Puerto Rico Travel Guide
> http://www.fodors.com/world/caribbean/puerto-rico/

Puerto Rico, World Factbook
> https://www.cia.gov/library/publications/the-world-factbook/geos/
> rq.html

absorb (ub-ZORB)—Soak up.

appetizer (AA-pih-ty-zer)—A small snack-type food that is served before the main meal.

colander (KAA-lun-der)—A bowl with many small holes that is used for draining water from foods.

colonist (KAH-luh-nist)—A person who moves to another land to live there.

cuisine (kwih-ZEEN)—A type of food from a certain place.

delicioso (dee-lih-see-OH-so)—"Delicious" (in Spanish).

discard (dis-KARD)—Throw away.

disposable (dih-SPOH-zuh-bul)—Able to be thrown away.

hearty (HAR-tee)—Containing plenty of nourishment.

legume (leh-GOOM)—A dry, one-celled fruit that splits naturally down the middle and is usually protected in a pod, such as peas and beans.

originate (or-IH-jih-nayt)—Come from; started.

panini (puh-NEE-nee)—A type of grilled sandwich made with flatbread.

prehistoric (pre-hiss-TOR-ik)—From the time before things were written down or recorded.

preserve—Taking action to keep something in its original state.

savory (SAY-vor-ee)—A flavorful food that is not sweet.

Amie Jane Leavitt is an accomplished author, researcher, and photographer. She graduated from Brigham Young University as an education major and has since taught all subjects and grade levels in both private and public schools. She is an adventurer who loves to travel the globe in search of interesting story ideas and beautiful places to capture in photos. She has written more than fifty books for kids, has contributed to online and print media, and has worked as a consultant, writer, and editor for numerous educational publishing and assessment companies. In addition to Amie's many other interests, she is also an avid cook and baker and a self-proclaimed "cultural foodie." Some of her favorite dishes come from countries and cultures far from her own. Amie particularly enjoyed writing this cookbook since it reminded her of the many fun times she has spent with dear friends who are from the Caribbean region of Latin America. To check out a listing of Amie's current projects and published works, visit her web site at www.amiejaneleavitt.com.